THE STRONG AND THE CRAZY EMPERORS OF THE ROMAN EMPIRE

Ancient History Books for Kids

Children's Ancient History

BABY PROFESSOR

EDUCATION KIDS

Speedy Publishing LLC

40 E. Main St. #1156

Newark, DE 19711

www.speedypublishing.com

Copyright 2017

The Roman Empire had an emperor at its head. Some did really well, and some were worse than bad. Read on about some of the best--and the worst--emperors Rome ever had.

FROM REPUBLIC TO EMPIRE

Rome started as little village, around 700 BCE. It became a kingdom, but after seven kings it became a Republic. A Senate of powerful, active leaders led the Republic for hundreds of years.

Ancient Rome

But the Republic became a victim of Rome's success. It seemed too slow and too awkward to keep Rome safe against enemies to the east and the north, and enemies within. Some people argued that the nation needed a single, strong leader.

There was a complicated civil war that seemed to be between the defenders of the Republic and those who wanted to change it. But it was really a struggle between powerful factions, each of which wanted to be in charge.

Julius Caesar

The first part of the civil war ended when Julius Caesar defeated Pompey in 48 BCE and became sole leader of Rome. But then Caesar was killed by those who feared his power in 44 BCE. After a second, long struggle, Octavian, Caesar's adopted son, became the sole leader of Rome in 27 BCE. He took the name "Augustus", which means "the great one".

HOW TO BECOME THE EMPEROR

There were three ways to become emperor, and none of them involved an election or being smart at running a country.

Crowning of Roman Emperor

BE OF THE EMPEROR'S FAMILY

If the emperor died, another family member would be likely to become emperor. This is the same pattern for kings and queens.

HAVE THE ARMY SUPPORT YOU

Sometimes a strong general would defeat the existing emperor, or seize the moment when an emperor died, and have his army proclaim him emperor. It sometimes took a lot of fighting for the new emperor to hold on to his title, and often he did not succeed

Roman Soldiers

BE WEAK AND LUCKY

Sometimes the army, or strong people in the court, would point to a weak or a young person in the imperial family and say, "Let's make him emperor!" Their idea was that the new emperor would be like a puppet and would do what the strong people or the army wanted.

THE BEST EMPERORS

AUGUSTUS
(27BCE-14AD)

Augustus brought an end to the Civil War and began the long era known as the Pax Romana--the time when the power of Rome ensured that cities would be safe, merchants could travel, and "barbarians" were kept under control. (Read the Baby Professor book Who Were the Barbarians? to learn more about them.) Augustus transformed Rome. He said that he had found it a city of brick and left it a city of marble.

Vespasian

VESPASIAN (69-79)

Vespasian was a good general and a great emperor. He restored Rome's fortunes after a series of bad emperors had led it to bankruptcy. He restored the power of judges and the courts, and made Rome stable again.

TRAJAN (98-117)

Trajan was a great general, and under him, Rome expanded to its greatest size. He also oversaw public building programs and an improvement in aid to the poor, to widows, and to those without resources. After Trajan, every new emperor got this wish from the Senate: may you be luckier than Augustus and even better than Trajan.

Trajan

Hadrian

HADRIAN (117-138)

Hadrian concluded that the Roman Empire had gotten too big to be defended, and that it needed shorter, more secure borders. In the north he build Hadrian's Wall at the frontier with what is now Scotland; in central Europe he established the Rhine River as the border. Hadrian was a scholar, a student of many subjects, and a very good architect. He also devoted a lot of attention to building up Rome's provinces, not just the center of the empire.

ANTONINUS PIUS
(138-161)

This emperor was both lucky and success-ful, in that during his long reign the empire enjoyed its greatest peace and prosperity. There were no major wars, no scandals in the emperor's household, and no natural or political disasters.

Antoninus Pius

Marcus Aurelius

MARCUS AURELIUS
(161-180)

Aurelius' generals defeated the Parthian Empire in the east, and many tribes in central Europe. He was a gifted philosopher and writer. He developed a theory of duty and service to the nation in works that scholars still read with appreciation.

SEPTIMIUS SEVERUS (193-211)

Septimius Severus defeated Germanic and African tribes so thoroughly that they did not cause trouble for Rome for the next hundred years. He conquered all of Mesopotamia, where Iraq and Iran now are. He was very popular with the common people and with soldiers, which the senators and the rich found some-what annoying.

Septimius Severus

Diocletian

DIOCLETIAN (284-305)

Diocletian recognized both external and internal pressures on the Empire. He created the "rule of four", with two co-emperors, each with an assistant, and each of the four governing one quarter of the Empire. The system worked very well, and for a while Rome was at peace again. It would stay largely intact for another hundred years. Diocletian was the first Emperor to retire without being forced to leave.

CONSTANTINE THE GREAT (307-337)

Constantine fought and won over enemies to the north, east, and west. He recognized Christianity and a legal religion. He established the eastern capital of the Empire, which he called after himself. Constantinople grew to be a powerful and beautiful city, and the Eastern Roman Empire continued there for a thousand years after the fall of the Empire in the West.

Constantine the Great

Tiberius

THE WORST EMPERORS

TIBERIUS (14-37)

Tiberius followed Augustus, but he did not really want to be emperor. He spent much of his time on the resort island of Capri and left the government of Rome in the hands of the Senate and of Sejanus, the head of the imperial bodyguard. On Capri, Tiberius followed decadent pleasures that would have shocked most Romans. In Rome, Sejanus accumulated power and wealth.

CALIGULA (37-41)

It is likely that Caligula was insane. He claimed to have been changed into a god, and demanded that the people of Rome worship him. He changed the heads of many statues of Roman gods, replacing them with busts modeled on himself.

Caligula

Caligula tried to make his favorite horse a Senator. He was randomly cruel, and entertained himself with torturing people in various ways. Caligula wasted all the money in the treasury, almost bankrupting the empire. Finally his own private guards stabbed him to death.

NERO (54-68)

Nero was a hateful, vicious man who had no concept of the needs of others. He divorced his first wife, had her head cut off, and gave the head as a gift to his second wife. He later became angry at his second wife and killed her, too.

Nero

While Nero was emperor, a huge fire burned much of Rome. The cost of rebuilding was huge, and Nero used extreme methods to get money from wealthy families. Finally the city had had enough, and Nero was forced to commit suicide.

DOMITIAN (81-96)

Domitian felt he had to keep himself in power by hurting anyone who might be his enemy. He invented new methods of torture. He condemned thousands of Christians to be torn apart by wild animals for the amusement of the audience in the Coliseum. Domitian started a war in Dacia, and mismanaged it so the campaign turned into a huge disaster.

Domitian

Commodus

COMMODUS (177-192)

Commodus thought that he was the reborn Hercules, and loved to fight against gladiators in the arena (the gladiators had inferior weapons and were handicapped in other ways). He once ordered the killing of all cripples and beggars in the city.

CARACALLA (198-217)

Caracalla was co-emperor with his brother, Geta. He wanted all power himself, so he surprised and killed his brother. He then killed or exiled anyone who objected to what he had done. When Caracalla heard that the citizens of Alexandria, in Egypt, had put on a satire making fun of him, he went with an army to Alexandria and had the troops attack his own city. More than 20,000 people died.

Caracalla

Maximinus Thrax

MAXIMINUS THRAX (235-238)

It seemed that this emperor wanted above all else to have everybody hate him. He did not trust anyone, and had most of his closest friends and most important advisors murdered. He started wars with nations that had not done anything against Rome. Finally, even his own guards had had enough. They killed him and his son and put their heads on poles.

HONORIUS (393-423)

Honorius was a hateful, jealous, racist. He offended his own people and neighboring Germanic tribes so much that the Goths attacked and pillaged Rome in 410. There is no good thing to say about this emperor

Honorius

Valentinian

VALENTINIAN III
(425-455)

Valentinian was another useless, jealous, and profoundly stupid emperor. Rome was fighting against several barbarian armies, and was succeeding under Genera Aetius. But Valentinian became jealous of how popular the general was becoming and had him executed.

THE WONDERS OF ROME

The Roman Empire was a complicated, glorious, corrupt, structure that lasted for hundreds of years. Read other Baby Professor books, like The Battles of Rome, The Role Families Play in Roman Culture and Society and The Golden Age of Roman Literature, to learn more about Rome.

Arch of Augustus

Visit

BABY PROFESSOR
EDUCATION KIDS

www.BabyProfessorBooks.com

to download Free Baby Professor eBooks
and view our catalog of new and exciting
Children's Books

Made in the USA
Lexington, KY
21 September 2017